IT'S NOT YOU

IT'S ME

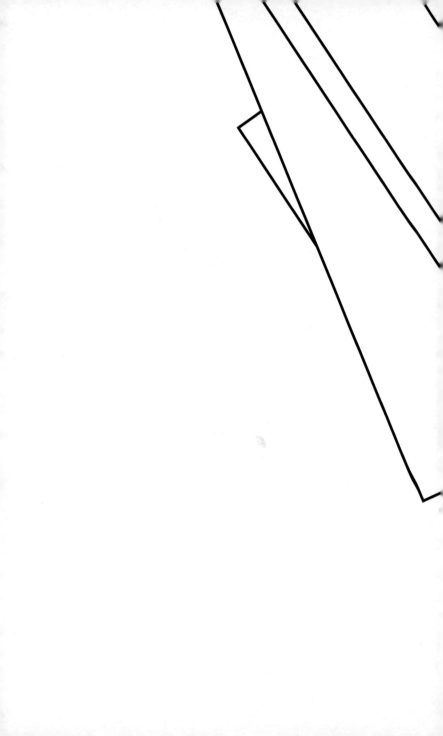

Mark Leruste

IT'S NOT YOU
IT'S ME

Break Up With Your Job, Make a Difference and Live a Life You Love

unconventional
hustler

"*If you're living a life that's not setting you on fire, you NEED this book.*"
Lisa Lister, author of *Sassy*

"*It took me six months to finally break up with my job before setting up my company; this book would have helped me to call bullshit and walk out the door a lot sooner.*"
Richard Patey, author of *Coffee Shop Entrepreneurs*

"*Mark is a perfect example of someone who takes life by the horns and forges his own path. If you're looking for career help that will ACTUALLY help you make changes in the right direction, read this book.*"
Rebecca Tracey, founder of The Uncaged Life

"*If you want to build the business and life you really want but are scared to leave your full-time job, "It's Not You, It's Me" will inject you with fear-busting energy!*"
Julie Leitz, Leadership coach

"*Reading Mark's book compels you to take the step you've been waiting too long to take.*"
Angus Fletcher, Founder of Streecoaching

"*This might be the best book on the subject ever written.*"
Michael Serwa, author of *From Good to Amazing*

"After reading this book from cover to cover in a single sitting I am chomping at the bit for the next opportunity to learn from Mark again."
Bridget Hunt, author of *Six Pack Chick*

"Don't read this book if you're expecting an easy time, Mark is going to make you work for your transformation into a more fulfilling life."
Kevin Boyd, author of *The Job Delusion*

"This read is a great nudge to go out there and start embracing a certainly more challenging but more rewarding path of life, and Mark Leruste delivers it in the most friendly, authentic and engaging way."
Naomi Thellier de Poncheville, Founder of ntp designs

"This book is for you if you feel stuck in your life, are unhappy and are looking for strategies to 'break free'. Mark's book teaches you how to embrace your fears, follow your dreams and start living the life you desire."
Jean-Pierre de Villiers, author of *77 Ways to Reshape Your Life*

"Mark, as a person, and in this book, braves calling bullshit on the excuses daring to stand between us and an infinitely more satisfying life. One where we can finally taste the greatness we bloody well knew we had inside us."
Alex Baisley, Founder of the Big Dream Program

"It's Not You, It's Me" gives you the hope and courage to cut loose and go after your dreams. Mark Leruste combines his skills as a no-bullshit storyteller, inspirational motivator and coach, showing you how to get off the job treadmill and find your way to a life of authenticity and meaning."
Saskia Fraser, author of *Raw Freedom*

First published in the United Kingdom in 2014 by
Unconventional Hustler.

info@unconventionalhustler.com | www.unconventionalhustler.com

A CIP catalogue record for this book is available from the
British Library

ISBN 978 0 9928808 0 4

Book Design: Leonardo Collina (www.leonardocollina.com)
Illustrations: Marichiel Ewert (www.inanutshellstudio.com)

Printed and bound in Great Britain by Orbital Print, Kent,
TN24 0GA on Greenpeace approved FSC certified paper.

*To those of you who at some point were told that
you couldn't achieve something based on your skills,
competencies, experiences or abilities; and still went for
it despite the fear of failure. I salute you for taking action
and journeying towards the unknown.*

This book is for you.

Mark Leruste

"I've always had infinite creative energy, a playful nature and the courage to be unconventional; but envious people prefer to call me nuts."
Jim Carrey

CONTENTS

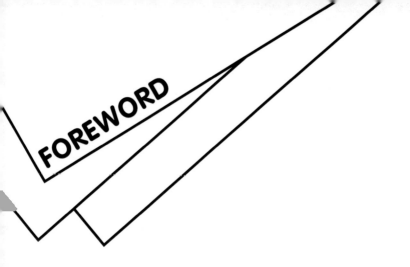

FOREWORD

> "If worrying about what people think of us is
> a limiting cage of our own making, telling our
> truth is the key to setting us free."
> Lisa Lister

Do you go to bed on Sunday evenings dreading what Monday holds for you? Do you hate your job and yet have no idea what you want to do instead? Do you feel unfulfilled at work? Do you feel like you should and, more importantly, could be doing something far more awesome? Yes? Then you're at the right place.

In 2012 I wrote an article titled 'Why You Should Break Up With Your Job' about following my quest to land my dream job while remaining *unfulfillingly* employed. To be honest, it was the first time I took a stab at really telling the truth about what was really going on in my life and what I was experiencing at the time. For once I dropped the politically correct bullshit and said what I was thinking; and I said it out loud. It turned out to be a blog post that resonated immensely with those who read it.

"It sounds like you're talking about me!"

"Yes! This is where I'm at right now too, thanks for sharing."

The emails and comments started to roll in, and that's when I realised I wasn't alone. I wasn't the only one feeling like I was stuck in a rut and unfulfilled at work. I wasn't the only one who felt like I was meant to be doing something else but just didn't know what that 'something' was. I wasn't the only one paralysed by fear and lacking the self-confidence to go after my dreams.

It wasn't that I didn't want to take action, change my career and do something different; I did. I just had no idea what that action should/would/could be. But now there were other people who, just like me, wanted to change up their careers but felt scared of the unknown. Scared to explore those 'Here Be Dragons' areas that we want to look at, but are too afraid to; the areas that stop us from living our most awesome lives.

'Here Be Dragons', a phrase coined by the American mythologist, author and lecturer Joseph Campbell, represents the places (both external and internal) that we are all afraid to visit. It could be the unknown consequences of quitting our jobs or it could be exploring certain emotions we've been hiding from for far too long. Just like in the Medieval days, when maps were drawn with serpents, dragons and mythical creatures marking areas to avoid, we let our dragons (or fears) dictate where we are willing, and unwilling, to go. But history has proven to us, time and time again, that it is those who are brave enough to venture where dragons dwell that go on to live lives filled with exciting and incredible adventures. And it is these brave people who eventually go on to explore and discover the world's deepest secrets and get to share their adventures with the rest of us.

No one should ever feel unfulfilled or unhappy at work.

And that's exactly why I've written this book. In these pages I've shared my own story-successes and failures included. I've answered the questions that I've been asked over and over by my friends and clients, and I've included several 'Try This' segments which I urge you to well, you know, try.

It's never too late to live your most awesome life. Unless you're dead, that is. Then it really is too late. So let's make sure you don't wait that long to take action.

Deal?

WARNING:

This book is not a dust collector or doorstop. Do not put this on the shelf. Its purpose it to help you create the radical shifts you want; be it quitting your current job to find your dream job, or launching your dream business. But for that to happen and for this book to have its desired effect, you need to read this book cover to cover within 48 hours of purchase. There's a reason you chose to buy it in the first place. And if you really want to make the most of this knowledge, the 'Try This' segments that I've included with recommended actions should be completed within 2 hours of reading this book. Are you ready to take on the challenge? Good. Get going. Your life and clock are ticking.

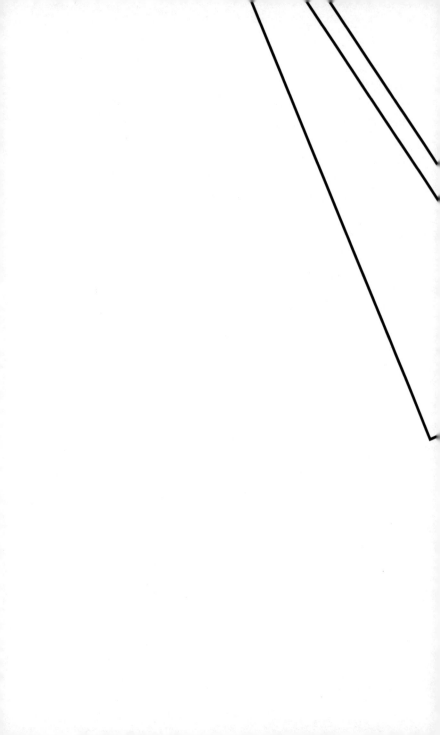

Chapter 1

THIS WAS NOT THE PLAN

"We must be willing to get rid of the life we've planned, so as to have the life that is waiting for us."
Joseph Campbell

Shortly after graduating from university with a business degree in 2007, I was what some might describe a 'success'. I travelled the world, interviewed CEOs and top governmental officials, saw my reports published in leading publications and co-founded an online suit-tailoring service for men that was featured in *The Wall Street Journal*.

But in 2009 my life took a turn for the worse. My personal life was a mess. I was heartbroken from a failing relationship and I found out that my grandfather had terminal cancer. I quit my job working for a company whose ethics I found questionable, ended my relationship and moved back in with my parents, seven years after leaving the family nest. I hit rock bottom.

I wandered a while in my attempts to numb the feelings of being lost and not knowing what to do with my life. To make things worse I couldn't find people who wanted to employ me because, according to them, I was over qualified for the positions I applied for. They feared that after my extravagant past I'd be 'bored' at these jobs.

I eventually teamed up with my childhood friend Denis Duvauchelle and co-founded Mister Tailor, an online suit-tailoring company. But the problem was that neither of us was making any money at that point. When my savings ran out I had no choice but to find a job. Any job.

I was out of cash and out of shape

After coming back to France from Peru, people thought I had eaten myself. I guess going from weighing 58 kilos in 2003 to weighing a staggering 81 kilos in 2009 didn't help dissuade them of this notion.

Eventually I found myself a 9–5 job sitting behind a desk at a business school in my hometown of Fontainebleau. I threw myself a month long pity party, which basically consisted of me blaming others for everything that was wrong in my life.

This was NOT the plan.

What had become of the young, ambitious, talented, creative and hungry young man that everyone had made me out to be? What had happened to the guy whose lifestyle and job seemed to be headed down a promising career path?

I started trying to bring about some change by searching hundreds and hundreds of blogs for tips and advice. I read everything from 'Why You Can't Find a Job You Love', 'When Is it the Right Time to Change Jobs?' and 'How to Find Your Passion.' I tried to get as much help as I could and I spoke with anyone willing to hear me out. I even tried a bunch of free online assessments to figure out what my perfect 'career fit' would be. But it kind of ended up feeling like I was reading my career horoscope. And as entertaining as it was, it wasn't really getting me anywhere. Despite all my efforts I still couldn't figure out what it was that I *really* wanted to do. I just couldn't see what my real path was meant to be.

Does my story sound familiar?

For a while I stayed in this state of flux; trying to figure things out, weighing my options, reading a thousand job descriptions and staying comfortable. Letting time slip by.

But I want to be clear about something - I didn't *hate* my job. My colleagues were lovely people and I was in a very fortunate position. I was working for a top global graduate business school with international perspectives. The pay was decent, and it was in my hometown. I was exposed to some incredibly interesting people, I got to save money and I was also able to spend a lot of time with my parents; a thing that had been a rare commodity for me over the past seven years while living abroad.

But I felt the same dissatisfaction and unease that I'd felt a few years ago while living the extravagant expat lifestyle. My job just didn't feel quite right. The work I was doing didn't feel in line with what I truly believed in or what was important to me, and I was desperate to do something more meaningful. I just knew there had to be a better fit for me, that there was more to life than this. There had to be. But what?

Like most people out there, I didn't know exactly what my dream job was, or how I'd get it. But that didn't matter. All I knew was that I needed to get out and find that dream job. A job that would have me feeling excited to get up in the morning; A job where I could do work that mattered and work that I loved; A job where I could work with the kind of people I loved spending time with. I didn't know what that job was, but I did know it definitely wasn't what I was currently doing. And that's the only thing I needed to know for sure in order to do something about it.

And then one hot summer morning, Wednesday 20th July, 2011 to be precise, while sitting at yet another mundanely boring sales meeting, I looked around the table and wondered to myself, *what the fuck am I doing here?* When I got back to my desk and saw a ton of emails pinging into my inbox - none of which I really cared about - I realised that that was it. I'd had enough. This was my breaking point where I knew I had to take action. So I sent a Facebook message to a friend and told him that I had to get out of my job. Fast. I knew he worked in the creative field, and I wanted in.

Don't give up

I've noticed that it's when things get tough that you know you're getting closer to your goal. That's when you know you're being tested to see how badly you want it. I didn't know what I wanted to do, but I knew what I didn't want to do. And I knew that I had to do something about it.

Life *will* throw punches at you. Question is; are you ready to take the hits while moving towards where you want to be? Mike Tyson once said, "Everyone has a plan until they get punched in the face." Punches will come your way, but the fact that you know they're coming puts you one step ahead of the game.

In 2013, Andy Murray ended Britain's 77-year wait for a Wimbledon men's singles champion with an epic three-set win over Novak Djokovic. Despite all his set-backs and previous losses, Andy persisted and didn't let life's punches wear him down. Instead he faced them with spirit and determination and eventually reached his goal.

TRY THIS

Stop thinking or talking about what you want to do, and take one step towards making it happen. Today. Make use of your support network. I'm sure you have friends you can reach out to. In fact, take a minute and think about it. Who do you know in your entourage that could help you on your quest?

Don't be afraid to also ask your friends and family if they know someone else that can help you out. Maybe they could help you write out your business plan, or help you pimp out your CV, or put a word in for you with someone who works at a company you love.

Reach out on Facebook asking if anyone in the industry you want to be involved in will let you take them out for coffee in return for a chat. It really doesn't matter what it is, just do something; anything that will take you one step closer than you were yesterday to your awesome life.

Closed mouths don't get fed - if you don't ask, you don't get.

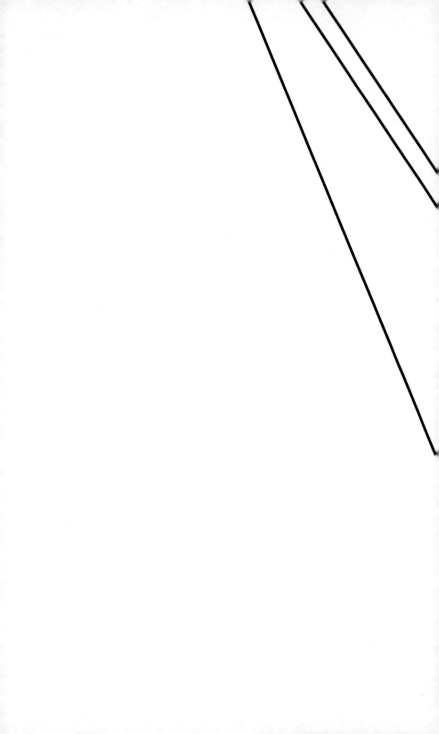

Chapter 2

ASKING FOR HELP

*"The strong individual is the one who asks for
help when he needs it."*
Rona Barrett

T he single most important decision I made at this particular
juncture of my life was to send out a rather desperate, and
some might even say slightly depressing, email to Roya Ferdows
from Life in Balance[1]. Roya is a Certified Professional Co-Active
Coach (CPCC), John Hopkins MBA graduate, Physical Trainer,
mother of two, a Taekwondo black belt and an overall *badass*.

She also happens to be someone who was around when I was a
very young child. She knew me when I still had a spring in my
step. And yes, she probably saw me running around naked, waist
down, in my big green boots when I was three years old.

There is no shame in wearing green boots.

This is an unedited copy of the email I sent to Roya on the
20th December, 2011:

> *'Dear Roya,*
> *I hope you are well. Surely this time of the year must be quite*
> *exciting in the US with Christmas around the corner. I write*
> *to you because I find myself once again at a cross road. Lost and*
> *confused. (That and the fact that I've been watching too many*
> *videos of Anthony "Tony" Robbins...) I could definitely use*
> *your help and guidance and I would love to hear your thoughts.*
> *Three weeks ago I took part in a mixed martial arts (MMA)*
> *tournament near Paris with only 2 weeks of real training (which*

was silly of me to do). Although I had joined the MMA gym in September, I had never done any competitive fighting before. So this was my first time. I obviously needed to prove something to myself. To be honest I was scared doing it, as no one in my MMA gym was doing it. I really didn't feel ready for it. But I didn't want to back out. So I went ahead with it; even though my coach was ill and couldn't come with me to the tournament. In short, I had two fights–I lost the first fight by points and the second fight cost me my right knee. I didn't tap out in time and my knee snapped. So I had to forfeit. Nothing too dramatic, just some twisted external ligaments. And I might have also damaged my meniscus, which could mean that I'll need surgery. I'll know for sure on the 26th after my MRI scan.

This really came as a huge blow to me as I had been trying to get back in shape for almost a year, and I was just starting to see some minor results. I was starting to feel good; in shape and a bit more confident. But now that I've been on crutches, unable to exercise and stuffing my face for a while, I'm almost back to square one. Which has made me feel down. And if I do have to have knee surgery, then I'm potentially out for at least 3 months and will have to wait 4–5 months before resuming any physical exercise :(

Even though I lost both fights, and potentially a knee in the process, I did learn something from this experience. I found out that I really loved the workout ethics and discipline (diet, physical exercise, etc.) behind training for a clear goal. And it really helped me put things in perspective. I've learned that hard work pays off. And that having a clear goal (in this case the tournament) helps you focus. People were willing to help me achieve that goal because I was motivated and determined to do it; even though I was terrified and under trained. Focus is good. It also made me love MMA and physical exercise even more. I loved learning and sharing the knowledge I was acquiring; by showing people at my gym exercises to help them reach their goals, or by showing my fellow partners at the MMA gym techniques I had learned online etc. It reminded me that I've always enjoyed coaching and sharing what I know to help people learn new things; whether in sports, business or life. It also reminded me how much I love healthy eating and physical exercise. When people started asking me for advice about nutrition and physical exercise it made me feel happy to help.

So why is all this important? Because I have been feeling down for quite some time and I'm fed up of it. I've been sleeping badly since 2009, feeling sorry for myself for a while, and the last time I remember being happy was in 2007. And that was when I graduated from uni with the grade I wanted (although I really didn't like studying business and suffered for it) and received a job offer which I thought was the best job in the world. Since then everything seems to have gone wrong.

Today I really feel stuck in a rut. Unhappy and, most of all, unfulfilled. I don't like my job, I'm bored out of my mind and I'm not doing any work at all. Most of the time I'm thinking to myself: "What the hell are you doing here? Take your stuff and go now!" I check my emails at least 10 times a day, spend way too much time on Facebook and look at stupid videos on YouTube. When I'm home I watch TV series and surf the net. This has taken a toll on my morale and on my relationship with my girlfriend as I have too much time to worry about silly things. I sulk about the fact I'm living back in Fontainebleau with a housemate that has no idea of what living in a shared accommodation means. I'm basically a substitute for his mum. Being a control freak probably doesn't help.

While all my friends are living in Paris, New York, Shanghai, London, I'm in Fontainebleau. I feel that I'm not doing what I should be doing. That I'm drifting far from my calling. Even though I'm good at sales, it's not what I want to do. I feel like I've gone backwards. That I was doing well and set for great things, but failed and fell a long way down. I feel dumber than ever before. My self-esteem is at an all-time low. I used to be a confident and happy child. Now I'm just mad at the world and mad at myself. I'm always angry and I rarely smile. And I don't like it. I used to believe that I was destined for greatness. That I was great at acting and communicating and that I was good with people. Now I just don't know how that's going to help me achieve what I want in life. I struggle getting up every day and dread the idea of going to work the next day. Sundays are the worst. I feel like packing it all in and setting off somewhere; maybe to travel to a foreign country to learn a martial art, or maybe just going back to study. I feel like I give up as soon as things get hard. I never finish anything; be it guitar, sports, business ideas or relationships. I never go the full nine yards.

I've also grown an interest to go back to school. Although at first I thought about doing an MBA, I quickly realised that I would hate it. I hate finance and accounting and the GMAT would just be pure torture. That said, I think I like the idea of having an MBA and think that having done an MBA would look pretty good on my CV. But I don't think that's what I should be doing. I'm a walking contradiction.

I'm sorry for the rant. I guess I needed to get it off my chest, and since you've known me for years (even though you haven't seen me in ages!) and because you're someone I trust and know is a life coach, I felt like sharing this with you.

FYI, I have been working on 'figuring out' what I want, what I'm good at, etc. for the past year or so. Doing a bunch of different exercises and tests. But I'm still not moving forward.

It was interesting watching videos of Tony Robbins, especially about reaching your goals in life. What I remembered is that there are three steps to reaching our full potential:

1. *Focus (the target): You need to have a target; be it for your body, business or relationships, etc. It has to be clear and you have to be able to say exactly what it is you want.*

2. *Get the best (tool box): Get the best out there; be it a coach, a book or some sort of teaching, etc. You need the best to help you learn and avoid wasting time with silly mistakes.*

3. *Resolve inner conflicts (80% of success in anything is your psychology, 20% is the mechanics). You know what you want and have the tools to get there, and yet you're stuck. This is because there is a conflict in you.*

So I guess I need to follow those three steps. But that's just the problem. I'm not sure I know what I want. And I always seem to make excuses.

Analysing my internal conflicts is also an issue.

*I read self-improvement books and they champion the idea
of just going for it. They talk about giving up what you're doing if
you don't like it, etc. But I'm still here. Still in Fontainebleau and
still at INSEAD[2]. A 6 month temporary option became a 2 year
permanent job. I know my parents mean well by saying,
"Stop complaining you've got a job. No one likes their jobs. You
should just feel lucky you're employed and have an income."
But I know there's more to life than feeling like this
right now.*

*I know that I should be looking at what is most important to me
today. I know that I can't look at life according to an old blue
print of what my friends, family, colleagues think. I might succeed,
but won't be fulfilled. I need to align my life with what's most
important to me.*

*"Clarity is power. What do you want? If you can't answer that
question in your personal life, body, business, etc. you're not going
to be fulfilled. […] Why are you doing it? Why? You need to have
enough emotional drive to break through that. […] Reasons come
first, answers come second."*

*I have at least discovered that I want to do something to
make a difference in the world. I'm really interested in social
entrepreneurship, coaching… I've been thinking of perhaps
becoming a coach? Or at least taking a course in coaching. Not sure
if you recommend me looking into this?*

*Wow sorry, that was a really, really long email. I really didn't
mean to go on for so long. I'm going to shut up now.*

---

2 The global graduate business school that I worked for from 2010–2012

I would love to hear your thoughts, and if you have any tips to share with me, that would be great. But I know it's Christmas season so you'll be busy.

Oh and if you want to read about my MMA tournament, here it is: http://www.adreamjobwouldbenice.com/2011/11/loosing-my-mma-virginity/

Thanks a million Roya.

Once again, sorry for the rant, if you don't have time to read my email or even reply not a problem at all. I totally understand! Take care and I wish you and all the family a fabulous Christmas and a very happy new year!

In hopes that 2012 is the year I take control of my life! :)

x Mark'

*"Freedom does not come automatically; it is
achieved. And it is not gained in a single bound;
it must be achieved each day."*
Rollo May

Following my email to Roya, she graciously took me on as
her coaching client, and played a crucial role in what was to
happen next.

Working with Roya I started to see that a good coach isn't there
to judge you or to make you feel bad about not achieving all the
things you want in life. They don't put pressure on you or add
things to your to-do list just for the sake of it. I realised that a
coach can help you get from where you are to where you want
to be in the most resonant way possible, while also making you
accountable for your own success.

While being coached by Roya I felt as if I was seen for the first
time, in a long time. Seen for who I was, and for what I could be;
and that in itself felt incredibly empowering.

Twice a month I got to spend an hour focusing on who I really
was and what I really wanted out of life. I was guided through
each sixty minute session as I explored my needs, my wants, my
dreams and my ambitions. Sure, it took some time to peel away the
layers of the emotional onion - past the bravado and past the fears
- but once we got to the core, that's when the magic happened.

Things became clearer. I started to understand that everything
was a matter of perspective. I realised that there wasn't just one

way of looking at things. There wasn't just one reality. In fact, I realised that there were many different ways of looking at a specific situation and feeling differently about it. I started to take ownership of my life. I realised that I was in charge of my decisions and that I did everything I did because I wanted to. Not because someone else was forcing me to. The day you realise this sublime fact is the day you can really start to change things up and create your most amazing life.

What coaching also did for me was that it gave me permission to be myself, and to accept myself for who I was and what I wanted to be; without having to apologise or feel guilty about it. And trust me, when that happened, it felt like a massive weight was lifted off my shoulders.

While working with Roya I also realised that I was truly passionate about making a difference in peoples' lives. Coaching quickly became a clear fit for me and I decided to venture on my own training course through the Coaches Training Institute (CTI)[3] to become an ICF (International Coach Federation) accredited CPCC. By doing this I knew I could too one day help others figure out their own journey.

Q. What if I can't afford a coach?

Before you pull the 'I can't afford it' card out of your pocket of excuses, ask yourself, "Is that really true?". If you go out and party during the weekend, or spend money on gadgets that only fill a material gap, then you have money to hire a coach. What's the price you've put on *yourself*? If you're spending all your cash on going out, numbing your senses with drink, drugs or junk food, or buying material add-ons in the hope your life will be better, then let me be blunt: you don't have your priorities right.

How much are you worth? I'll tell you-you are priceless.

Imagine what would have happened if the Olympians who took part in the London 2012 Olympics didn't have a coach in their corner. They would never have made it to the Olympics. Sure, they're talented athletes and they may have even won some of their events. But no records would have been broken and I seriously doubt we'd have seen the level of performance that we were all in complete awe of. That's why every single Olympic medallist, every top athlete, and every single world champion, in any discipline, has a coach; pushing them, believing in them and moving them through their comfort zone to reach their personal best. Someone that helps them to foresee obstacles, face their fears and roots them on towards success.

Although I wasn't shooting for a gold medal, having a coach made me feel like I had someone in my corner that believed in me; Someone who was pushing me to reach my own personal best and my own level of awesome; Someone who didn't let me make excuses, and someone who held me accountable for my own actions. I felt that I had someone who was truly on my side, no matter what.

Hiring a coach isn't an absolute necessity. But it IS a game-changer and it can mean the difference between getting a good job and landing your dream job. It can also mean the difference between starting a business that's OK, and starting a business that helps you wake up burning with passion each day. It's your call.

TRY THIS

Hire a coach. And if hiring a coach just isn't an option right now, look out for the numerous coaches who give away a heap of free stuff online that can move you forward on your personal pursuit of an awesome life. Read their blogs, sign up to their newsletters and look for those that provide free consultations or free sample sessions so you can get a taste of what coaching is all about. Make sure the coach you hire is a good fit though. You'll know pretty much straight away if you click with their style or not.

Here are some of my favourite coaches that share free resources online:

• Lisa Lister–www.sassyology.com

• Rebecca Tracey–www.theuncagedlife.com

• Corrina Gordon-Barnes–www.youinspireme.co.uk

• Tad Hargrave–www.marketingforhippies.com

• Marie Forleo–www.marieforleo.com

Chapter 3

THE 'I DON'T KNOW WHAT TO DO' CLUB

"The two most important days in your life are the day you are born and the day you find out why."
Mark Twain

I f I had a penny for every time I heard a client, friend or someone I know tell me, "I don't know what I want to do, that's the problem." I'd be a very, VERY rich man.

There was a point when I wasn't sure what the hell I wanted to do with my life either. At one point I flirted with the idea of becoming a real-life version of Don Draper from *Mad Men*. I even scored an interview with Newhaven, an advertising agency based in Edinburgh. They were hip, cool and quirky, but I didn't get the job. My Don Draper dreams were dashed, and I sulked.

The problem here was that I wasn't clear about exactly what it was that I wanted to do. I was taking action and the universe definitely rewarded me for it. But I really needed to gain clarity about what I *truly* wanted to do. Not just, "That sounds nice; I could do that," but rather, "Oh my God! I freakin' love this shit!"

Q. But what if I don't know what to do?

Welcome to the world's biggest club!

The simple fact that you are questioning yourself on this fact means that there's a pull, a hunger for something, and that's a great sign. I believe that we are both blessed and cursed to live during this particular period of time. Cursed because there are literally thousands, if not millions, of various opportunities and choices we can pursue, making it all too complicated to commit to one thing. For instance, we can live anywhere in the world and we can pretty much do any sort of work we want if we put our mind to it. And this means that it's never been more difficult to choose what we really want to do. It's like being in a sweet shop the size of an Olympic stadium and being told that you can only have one type of candy. Just one. Where do you start? Which one do you choose? *They all look amazing, why am I only allowed one?* We're conditioned to seek safety and to seek security, which is why we feel inclined to reach for the tried and tested jobs. The ones that come with clear and well-defined paths. But there are so many jobs around us, including working for ourselves which can be so much more appealing and fulfilling. And yet we get in our own way.

If you have any doubts about making a living doing something that isn't being a lawyer, a banker, an accountant, a corporate director, or an advertising executive, simply take a look at anyone who has become a successful social entrepreneur, conscious solopreneur, life coach, personal trainer, author, nutritionist, masseur or yoga instructor. Success isn't what your parents thought it meant. Technology has made it easy to build a meaningful business with a global reach from the comfort of your own kitchen table.

You can build a community/tribe/crew of like-minded people who love what you do and are willing to pay you for doing it. I've come to call them *The Awesome Crew*. These are the people who you LOVE connecting with and the people who love connecting with you.

In his book *Tribes: We Need You to Lead Us*, Seth Godin explores the concept of tribes in greater detail. I highly recommend that you pick Seth's book up and give it a read.

Corrina Gordon-Barnes also talks about her 'Love, Love, Money Tribe' in her book *Turn Your Passion to Profit: A Step-by-step Guide to Getting Your Business off the Ground*. These are all great examples and resources to learn how you can make a living (and then some) doing what you love.

Q. How do you choose what to do?

What if you could do anything? No matter how ludicrous or impossible it may seem, what if you could do it? Drop the *'I don't know'* line. You DO know. Reach into that burning core within you. What's there? Saying 'I don't know' is the easy way out. It's a self-protection mechanism that kicks in when you want me to leave you alone and stop prodding you for answers; quite possibly because you're scared of what might come up.

But I dare you. Close your eyes[4]. Take a deep breath in and let it out. Allow yourself to dream big. Who do you really want to be?

I DON'T KNOW

Forget about what you want to do for a second. But think about who you want to be. Do you want to be a person that inspires teenagers to love themselves for who they are and not for what they look like? Do you want to be an explorer travelling around South East Asia and filming documentaries about martial arts and local fighters? Do you want to be a teacher that guides women on how to unleash their super powers so they can go and make a change in the world?

4 For my audio guided version of this exercise
  visit www.markleruste.com/book/bonus

Then you can start thinking about what you want to do. I don't care what limitations you have put upon yourself in order to play small. That is not how we roll around here. Viktor E. Frankl wrote in his ground breaking book *Man's Search for Meaning: The Classic Tribute to Hope From the Holocaust:* "Live as if you were living for the second time and had acted as wrongly the first time as you are about to act now."

This is your one shot at telling the universe what it is you *really* want. I'm not interested in the *'Yeah, but that will never work'* line either. This is not the time for that voice. This is the time for the voice of opportunity and hope. Have you got something? Anything? Good.

Now say it out loud. Sing it out loud. Shout it out loud. How does it feel? Is it scary? Is it funny? Is it ridiculous? Good. Those are all signs that you're not comfortable with the idea, which in turn is an indication that you need to go explore it further. It needs to be so big that it's silly. Now, let's say that you've decided you want to have your own TV show where you talk about your favourite recipes for tasty and nutritious meals that have changed your life. What are the first steps you need to take? The most practical first step is to start taking a look at anything similar out there. But remember, when we compare ourselves to so-called 'celebrities' or 'successful' people, we have a tendency to feel intimidated rather than inspired. So hold back on the comparison, and instead get curious about understanding what they've achieved and how they've achieved it. Study them. Know that they too once started at ground zero. There is no place for any "Oh, but I'll never be as good as X" or, "What's the point? It's already being done by X," bullshit.

It doesn't matter that other people have done it or are still doing it, you are YOU, and are capable of bringing your own flavour to the mix. Do great marathon runners stop running because there are other great marathon runners in the world? Hell no. They train harder, keep on running and keep on competing.

A few months ago, I was doing this exercise with a wonderful guy named Sean who was working for a global blue chip company at the time. He realised that the nature of the work he was doing, coupled with working in a big corporate environment, just wasn't the right fit for him. Sean hated the way people were being treated and were being exploited at his work place. The poor management skills displayed by his supervisors really got to him. He lived out of hotel rooms and was working ridiculously long hours. Commuting back and forth by plane every weekend wasn't fun either. He wanted more time to do the things he loved, like developing phone apps, working out and eating healthily. He wanted to explore something completely different and try something completely new. As a result, Sean eventually quit his job and joined a promising start-up team in Amsterdam to help them develop their mobile app to be pitch-ready for investors. Even though Sean had no previous experience in developing mobile apps, he knew he wanted to help small teams reach a wider audience by developing kick-arse apps. So he started small and slowly taught himself how to develop an awesome mobile app for Twoodo[5], and was subsequently asked to join the start-up full time to further develop their mobile app. Oh and Sean no longer lives out of a suitcase and is able to fit in his workouts during any time of his day.

TRY THIS

Write down five things that scare you. It could be to dance in the middle of the street, scream out loud in the middle of a park, ask someone you like out on a date, or to just speak in front of an audience. It could even be something as simple as smiling at someone during your daily commute. It doesn't matter what it is, just write down five things that really leave you feeling uncomfortable or ridiculous. Something that would make you think, *'No way, I can't do that!'*

Now pick one thing off the list you've just made and do it. I dare you.

That's right; I'm asking you to man (or woman) up and do something that you're afraid of doing. Start with the least intimidating thing on your list and work your way up. For example, as a child I used to be a very opinionated kid, and I was the cheekiest little fellow in my school. But as I grew up I let people chip away at my confidence and I started to fear confrontation the same way I fear gigantic (hairy) spiders. So I started to work on this and practised standing my ground in conversations with people I was comfortable with. This initially included my parents, my brother and my closest friends. I knew that they'd love me no matter what I'd say, and that I could trust them to still be there for me, even after telling them how I actually felt about certain things.

After I started practising with my family and friends I moved on to practising on other people around me: colleagues, acquaintances, housemates and eventually, clients. I'm still building my confidence in confrontational situations and I still catch myself being weary at times; but I've learned how liberating it can feel to slay one of my dragons.

And as Anthony Robbins often says: "If you can't, you must. And if you must, you can." So go on and get started!

NEED A HAND?

If you feel like you could use some extra encouragement when doing this, get in touch at *facebook.com/markleruste* and tell me about your sticking points. And after you've taken on your fears you can report back to me on how it went, so that we can celebrate together!

Chapter 4

FAIL FORWARD

"There is only one thing that makes a dream impossible to achieve: the fear of failure."
Paulo Coelho

Have you ever wondered what lies behind fear? I'm no expert, but what I've learned from talking to dozens, if not hundreds of established and budding entrepreneurs over the years is that there's another big word behind the word fear. The F word. No not that, silly. I mean Failure[6]. Failure is a taboo in our society. It's often frowned upon and sometimes used as a measure of self-worth. It's something we've never been taught to embrace, love and respect.

What will people say? How will they react? What will happen if...?

All these questions come in to play and suddenly, our most awesome life becomes obsolete. We're too busy focussing on how to limit the damage and avoid pain to get anywhere near success. But what you need to realise is that failure comes with a gift that most of us do not see, or appreciate.

I've experienced rejection more times than I'd like to admit. At one point in my life I was so tired of spending my evenings scouting for job openings and spending my weekends applying for them. I must have easily applied for over a hundred jobs and been interviewed for at least a dozen of them. But none of them felt *right*. The closest I got to accepting a gig that I thought could be my dream job was when I interviewed for the role of Editorial Content Manager at an editorial agency in Paris. Although I'd made it through the intensive four-round interview processes, and got a job offer, I knew something wasn't right.

In fact, from the moment I walked into the office I knew that it didn't feel right. I couldn't put my finger on what it was exactly, but I kept trying to rationalise the decision process and make myself believe that it would be a great opportunity. *It's a change Mark. What else are you going to do? You've got a job offer, take it!* But deep down, I knew something was wrong. I knew I wanted more than a cubicle job where I was stuck behind a computer screen pushing out content for companies I didn't believe in (I had to re-write a press release for a famous global nuclear company as a writing test to get through one of the four rounds of the interview process. Although I passed, needless to say, I had no interest in the subject, whatsoever).

The night before giving them my final decision I remember having a chat with my dad who, by the way, isn't the most emotionally accessible person. During that particular phone call he told me that if I wasn't excited or jumping out of my seat to take on the job, and didn't 'feel' it, then I should probably drop it.

So I did. And I am SO glad I did because it would have been just another sticky plaster over my not-so-dream-job situation. And besides, I would have missed out on what was to come.

Reengineer your fears

In 2013 my friend Jean-Pierre de Villiers [7] gave me a spare ticket to a Tim Ferris[8] talk. I got to meet Tim after his presentation and I asked him what he thought about failure-I was due to give a talk the following Saturday at event on the most crucial challenges that budding entrepreneurs face, and I thought I could really use Tim's input. Tim told me that, "Failure is feedback." He went

6 Visit www.markleruste.com/book/bonus to download your free
  audio recording of my keynote speech: 'The F Word'
7 www.jpdvglobal.com
8 Author of The New York Times Best Seller *The 4 Hour Work Week*

onto explain how his scientific background helped him put his entrepreneurial failures into perspective and realise that setbacks don't mean the end of the world. He said that he looks at failures as just another opportunity to adapt and try again until he found something that works. Tim understands that there is always a solution out there and that it's just a matter of failing the required number of times before finding it. Amen to that, Tim.

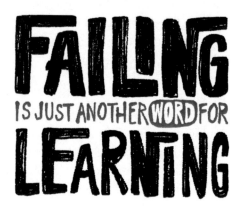

On meeting Tim

Meeting Tim after his presentation wasn't as easy breezy as I might have made it sound. This is how it really went down:

After his presentation, Tim did a Q&A session for 90 minutes. I kept on raising my hand throughout the whole session but didn't get noticed. So when Tim called out that the next question was going to be the last, instead of sitting there with my hand raised like everyone else, I stood up and waved my hands like a cheerleader. Everyone laughed and my heart was racing. Tim just smiled and said, "Yeah not you," and picked someone else. I was gutted! I had showed initiative and he had turned me down. Publicly. But I was determined to get my question answered.

After the Q&A session wrapped up Tim did a book signing session, and the queue was quite honestly MASSIVE! I thought of leaving, but just as I was about to, I thought to myself, *you'll regret this later on, won't you?* So I bought a copy of his latest book *The 4-Hour Chef* (despite me already having a copy back home) and took my place in the queue. After what seemed like ages, I got to the front of the queue. But I was rushed through and I didn't get the chance to ask Tim my question.

Just as I was being ushered away, I noticed the exit doors that Tim was most likely to leave through. So in true stalker fashion I lurked around the door until Tim was ready to leave and popped in front of him with my question. A lot of people might call me crazy but, hey, I got to meet Tim Ferris in person!

Q. But failing sucks. I'd rather do nothing than risk failing, that's an option isn't it?

Yes, it is. But if you want to create the most awesome life you need to make fear your bitch and risk failure. Often.

TRY THIS

Draw a circle on a piece of paper and title it 'Here Be Dragons'. Next list out your 'dragons'or fears in that circle. Take a good look at them and then go ask a four year-old what he or she thinks of your list. Or try to imagine what your four year-old self would think of these fears. When I did this exercise I realised that my four year-old self would have laughed at my list of fears and told me that it's not that big of a deal.

It's time to slay those dragons, once and for all.

The bottom line is this: as long as you know and believe that at the end of the tunnel lies your Promised Land, it's all worth it.

Because no matter what, you should never settle for anything less than what you deserve. Don't let opinions, thoughts or insecurities, be it your own or of others around you, stand in the way of your dream job, passion project or ultimate business.

No matter how hard it gets, or how low you feel, remember that this will only make you stronger. It will test your worth and show you what you're really capable of. And you know what? All of your experiences, obstacles and failures will become great content for your future bestselling autobiography–it's a win-win situation.

Q. But I fear the unknown, how do I deal with that?

Mankind has always been afraid of the unknown. It's in our nature. Our animal instincts kick in when a bush rustles, and we fear the sabre tooth tiger that might jump out of it. Even if that rustle was just the wind.

I'm not going to tell you that the unknown isn't scary, because it is. But you have to take action; you have to step up anyway. In my video interview *Fighting Fear with Daniel Terry*[9], Daniel, who is the World Muay Thai Council MAD European Champion, mentions that it's healthy to have a bit of fear. He says that every single fighter, no matter how skilled or how well-prepared, still has some sort of fear before a big fight. But you should never let that little voice-that little saboteur-take control of your actions or feelings.

9 The full video interview is available online at www.youtube.com/markleruste
   (Video production credits: Gus Newsam (www.gusnewsam.com))

Les Brown puts it this way:

*"Too many of us are not living our dreams
because we are living our fears."*

Ask yourself this: what's the worst that could happen? In fact, take a minute to write down your darkest worst-case scenarios. Be as pessimistic and morose as you can. Now look at your list head-on, stand up, and say, "Fuck you. I'll do it anyway!" I'm not saying that you can jump off a bridge without a parachute and expect to have an easy fall. What I'm saying is that you can tackle your fears by understanding where they're coming from. Are they coming from a place of doubt? Are you making them seem bigger than they really are? Are you making a mountain out of a mole hill? Be honest with yourself.

Next I want you to write down at least two fail safes that you can fall back on should your worst-case scenarios materialise. Could you go back and live with your parents? Could a friend help you out for a few months?

I can't promise you that your business will be a success or that you'll find your dream job just by taking action. But I can promise you that if you don't take action, you'll never get a chance to know how successful your business might have been, or to find out what your dream job could have been. As Sam Tittle, founder of TheCoffice.biz puts it in Richard Patey's book *Coffee Shop Entrepreneurs: Wake Up and Smell the Location Independent Economy*: "If your job looks good on paper but never quite feels like the right fit then you should probably get off the hamster wheel and figure out what isn't working for you."

Stay put, or be in action. The choice is yours. People have walked this path of uncertainty before you and I, and they too have been as scared as we are.

Are you scared of telling your boss that you want to leave your job? Are you afraid of what might be in store for you once you step outside the confines of your safety zone? When you're a baby you first crawl, then you stumble, and then you walk, right? Well, it's pretty much the same throughout life. Sometimes we walk, sometimes we fall over and sometimes we get rejected. But when we grow a pair and get courageous our 'can do muscle' gets some serious action. You can even start off small by simply saying no to an invitation you really don't want to accept, but usually would just to keep the peace. There might be some initial ripples because people aren't used to you standing up for yourself. But when you realise that the world doesn't implode, and that no one likes you any less for putting yourself first you'll become addicted to the feeling of brave decisions and you'll start to develop your intuition for what's right and wrong on your way to success.

TRY THIS

The next time you want to talk to someone about something that feels uncomfortable-maybe your colleague hasn't pulled their weight at work or your housemate's forgotten to do the dishes or your boss has just put you down in front of everyone for no valid reason-instead of backing off or ignoring it, push yourself into having a conversation about it.

The following exercise based on the Non Violent Communication Model[10] that I discovered during my ORSC (Organization and Relationship Systems Coaching)[11] fundamentals course is a great way to go about having these hard conversations.

Start by describing the situation.

"Hey, you know on Tuesday when we talked about where to go on holiday this summer?"

Then describe what happened without any personal opinion.

"And you mentioned that it was either Spain or nowhere…"

Now describe how that made you feel.

"Well I felt like you were leaving me no option but to pick your choice, when I feel like we should be picking a place that we both feel enthusiastic about. That really made me feel insignificant."

Describing how you feel is very different from accusing the other person of something they did. People can't criticise you for feeling what you feel. It's not an opinion, it's a feeling. In fact, you'd be surprised at how little people know about how their actions sometimes make others feel. So letting them know is actually an eye-opener for them.

Finally, wrap it up by explaining how you'd like it to play out next time.

"I'd really appreciate it if the next time we talk about our summer holiday, we both get to express our options and discuss where we'd both like to go to without giving each other ultimatums."

Notice how all of a sudden it's less scary to talk about something that initially might sound really bad? And what's great about this method is that you can apply it in almost any situation; be it a business meeting, a talk with friends or a disagreement with your partner.

10 www.nonviolentcommunication.com
11 www.centerforrightrelationship.com

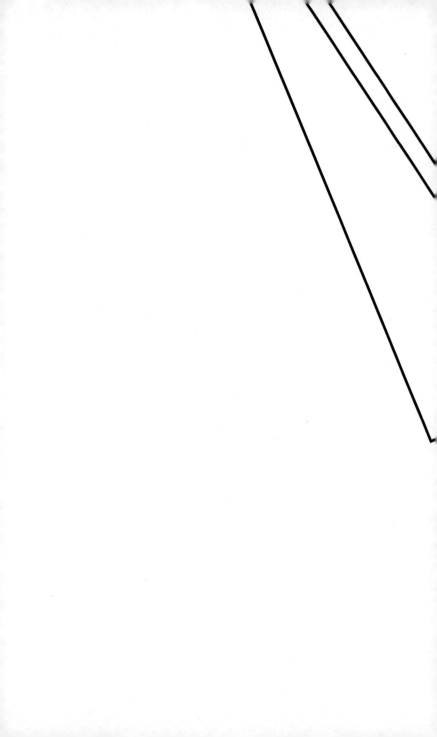

Chapter 5

DARE TO BE DIFFERENT

*"First they ignore you, then they laugh at you,
then they fight you, then you win."*
Mahatma Gandhi

Y ou know how sometimes you come up with a crazy idea and
the people around you laugh, frown, or try to shoot it down
immediately? Well that's exactly how this all started. I had a crazy
idea and people *did* laugh at it, and *they* did try to shoot it down,
but for some reason - intuition/foolishness/blind faith - I went
right ahead with it anyway.

Being dyslexic I've always had to find ways to adapt to the world
around me by doing things a little more creatively. I've never seen
this as a disability, but rather as a gift. I grew up in France, and the
education system there wasn't exactly cut out for multicultural,
curious, buzzing, creative kids with loads of energy to spend. As
a result I spent most of my childhood dreading spelling tests,
missing school as much as possible and trying to figure out how I
could fit in a system that just wasn't made for me. I was constantly
being put down and publicly humiliated in class by most of my

teachers. I struggled in maths, science and language classes, but excelled in drama, sports, art and history. Thinking back on that time reminds me of something my amazing friend and colleague Julie Leitz[12] once said: "It felt like I was a piece of a puzzle that ended up in the wrong set. There was no way I was going to fit in." But on the plus side, these early years also meant that I had to accept and embrace the fact of being *different*. And I'm all about being different.

That's why I knew I would never land my dream job smack bang in the middle of a financial crisis if all I had in my arsenal was a boring and conventional CV; especially seeing as I'm not that great at writing. In fact my writing used to be downright terrible. But through militant practice and by putting myself and my words out there on the big wide web. I've improved over the years; enough to produce this book, in fact.

So you see anything is possible. Results and success might not be instant; they take time, patience and dedication, but if you're willing to do the work the universe will eventually reward your actions.

Bruce Dickinson of Iron Maiden once said, "There are many talented musicians in the world, but determination is the key to success. There aren't as many determined people in the world as there are talented ones."

During my career meltdown I reached out to one of my friends named Andreas to help me find a job. He suggested that I look into a role available at his creative ad agency, but also gave me a warning: "Sending a CV in doesn't really have much of an effect in

12 www.julieleitz.com

a lot of cases. There always has to be an innovative way in for him *(i.e. his boss)* to see that you are right for the job and the agency. I'm happy to pass your CV on but you're better off thinking about what else you can do to get his attention..."

Andreas' advice not only pushed me to explore alternative ways of packaging myself while on my quest for a job I loved, but it also reaffirmed my belief that I had to come up with something different to stand out. That very day I decided to come up with an online resume that encompassed all my skills and past experiences. The only problem was that I had no idea what it would look like or how I'd make it happen.

Although I was eager and willing, I knew I couldn't do it on my own. I wasn't a big fan of asking people for help at the time, because it made me feel needy and awkward, but I was surrounded by a wealth of knowledge too powerful to ignore. And I was lucky enough to have a bunch of friends with amazing skills who wanted to support me.

So even though I wasn't sure if they would accept, I put myself out there and I reached out to them asking for help. I explained to them that I was hurting, and that I wanted out of my current job. There were a few that laughed and shot the idea down, but there were others who said that if their skills could help me land my dream job, then they'd be more than happy to help out.

One such person was my brother-from-another-mother Denis Duvauchelle[13] who helped me build my website. I needed to show prospective employers what I was made of and I knew a paper CV was just not going to cut it. I knew that I rock out at talking, so I decided to create a video CV. I wanted to change careers and start working in a creative industry, so I had to show my prospective employers that I wasn't just another corporate heartless sell-out. I approached the incredibly talented Mickey Mahut[14], who also happened to be a childhood friend of mine, to help me make my video CV idea a reality. With Mickey ready to help me with the filming and editing, I immediately set about writing the script, scouting for locations and enlisting the help of other friends who were up for being featured in the video as extras.

Despite what the majority of people around me thought about my idea at the time, including my parents, I launched a fully-fledged online dream-job-hunting campaign called 'A Dream Job Would Be Nice!' (www.adreamjobwouldbenice.com). The idea was to integrate everything I'd ever done career-wise into one multimedia platform.

But my video CV wasn't produced in a day; in fact, it took a few months to get it up to a standard that truly rocked. But after a few hundred hours of hard work, the website was live and running with my video CV.

Q: Why did it take months?

Well, for starters, I must have written the script over a hundred times. Should it be funny? Should it be serious? Should it be all about me? Should it be about what I do? I was also letting myself be influenced by what other people thought. One person was telling me to do one thing: "Video CVs don't work, they make you sound and look like a douche bag" or "It can't be too funny, it's a CV after all", while another was telling me to do it completely differently: "Don't take yourself too seriously, it should be light

13 www.denisduvauchelle.com
14 www.dailymotion.com/yabox

hearted and funny!" I got so confused that I almost ended up not doing it at all.

At one point in 2011, Denis Duvauchelle sent me a link to the video CV of Matthew Epstein, an American guy trying to land himself a job at Google. It was pretty funny and looked a lot like what I had in mind. Denis had come across it and thought that sharing it with me would encourage and inspire me on my journey to produce my own video CV, especially since this guy's video had thousands of views in just a couple of weeks. But it totally backfired. I felt devastated. I felt like someone had beaten me to the punch. I felt that I would now be perceived as a fraud and a copycat, even if I had come up with the idea myself before I had ever heard of this guy's video CV.

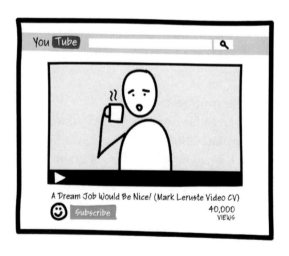

But in the end, Mickey Mahut gave me the best advice. He reminded me that I was different, that my background was different and that my video CV was going to be different too. And then he added the crucial line that made it all happen: "We just need to shoot. If we don't, it will never happen." He was right.

There's a time for talking about your project (motion), and there's a time for actually getting it done (action)[15]. I probably could have done it all in a month had I been better organised and more focused. But I wasn't, and it cost me precious time.

---

15 Read *The Mistake Smart People Make: Being In Motion Vs. Taking Action* by James Clear–http://jamesclear.com/taking-action

chapter 6

GROW A PAIR.
BALLS OR OVARIES,
YOU CHOOSE

*"I learned that courage was not the absence of
fear, but the triumph over it. The brave man
is not he who does not feel afraid, but he who
conquers that fear."*
Nelson Mandela

Did you know that most of our adult life-roughly one third of it in fact-is spent at work? So why would you want to spend one third of your life working in a job you don't like? Would you want to spend one third of your life with a person you didn't like or enjoy being around? Just so you know the answer should be a big, fat *no*. But sometimes self-doubt can creep in and self-doubt sucks.

While it's perfectly normal to doubt yourself, sometimes it can be too easy to just listen to the negative voices around us, including our own, and give up. If you find yourself realising that what you're doing just isn't doing it for you anymore, I dare you to do something drastic to kick-start your life. If you're not happy where you are and you know you shouldn't be there; then break up with your job. Hand in your notice saying you'll leave in a month, or in three months, or in whatever amount of time your employment contract states. This should give you enough time to secure your finances and move on to your next big thing; be it your dream job or your own kick-arse business. At the very least this will force you to get your arse off the chair and step into action.

I originally uploaded my video CV as a password-protected video on Vimeo[16] so I could hand pick those who could see it. But when I decided to make my video CV live and public on YouTube in January 2012, I was starting to panic that I'd made a mistake. I thought that maybe those around me were right to say that I was crazy and that I was putting myself at serious risk by openly being on the lookout for a new job while still being fully employed. I thought I was probably being unreasonable and that maybe I should just stick to the job I had, be content with it, and drop the whole idea of chasing my dream job before someone at work caught me 'wanting out'. The fact that I filmed some of the scenes from the video CV at my workplace at the time didn't help with my worries either. And then on one idle Tuesday afternoon in January, a girl I knew from another department at work burst into the office open space, where my manager was also working from, and shouted, "I just saw your video, I LOVE IT!" My heart just dropped and I started panicking. I gave her the big owl eyes and tried to make her understand that this wasn't cool. I tried to cover things up by saying, "Oh yeah, my skateboarding video when I was 15? Yeah that was a long time ago eh?" And thank God she got it and sheepishly closed the door. She immediately sent me an email to apologise for not thinking it through.

By that point fear was slowly but surely creeping in and trying to sabotage my courage to take action. But I quickly shook that gremlin off and stuck with the plan. I just knew deep down that I had to do something and that it was eventually going to pay off. It just had to.

You just can't foresee what is ahead of you.

Thinking that you can see the future is insane. Unless you're the inside of a fortune cookie, there is no way you can predict what's going to happen in your future. Unless you have a car that can take you *Back to the Future*; in which case you need to drop me a line so that we can go for a spin together. For real.

TRY THIS

Start small, but start something. Don't stay stuck in the dream room for too long. Because the quicker you get out there and start trying out your dream and vision for size, the quicker you'll be able to adopt it and change it up to make sure it fits you perfectly.

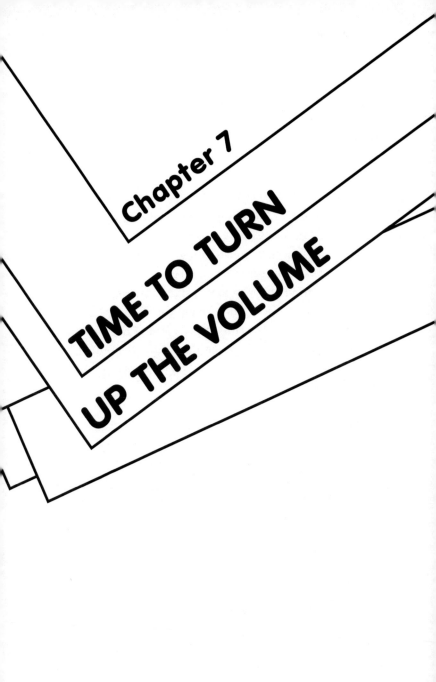

Chapter 7

TIME TO TURN
UP THE VOLUME

"Take the first step in faith. You don't have to see the whole staircase, just take the first step."
Dr. Martin Luther King Jr

W hen I read *The Job Delusion: How to Start Thinking Your Way to Financial Freedom!* by my friend and colleague Kevin Boyd, it reminded me of just how much we tend to hand over the keys of our financial security to our employers. Sure it's convenient while it lasts; we can count on a regular pay check coming in each month. But what would happen to you should your organisation decide to terminate your job? How would you feel? And how long could you survive before you officially had to declare yourself broke? Weeks? Months? That's when I had an 'aha' moment. My relationship to money and how I perceived what job security meant to me had to change.

In today's fast-paced and ever changing economy I believe that we can no longer rely on our jobs to guarantee our employment or financial security. It just isn't sustainable in the long run. I believe that we are going through a social entrepreneurship revolution, where people are no longer driven by the figure on their pay-checks at the end of the month but rather by the impact and the difference their work is making on the world.

"An entrepreneur accepts that the world is the way that it is and goes about changing it rather than waiting for someone to make it easy for them."
Richard Reed

That's why we need to find new ways to generate multiple revenue streams so we can go out and do the work that we love without having to worry about our money tap running out. And that's why I spent more than four years building side businesses, while being fully employed, before taking the big leap. It wasn't easy, but it proved that I wanted it bad enough to make it work.

When you get up at 5am to start working on your website, product, service, or business, and then come back home from your full time job at night and still find the energy and motivation to work on your business well into the night; you know you've got the determination and heart to see it through. It's not easy, if it was everyone would do it. But that's also why it's such an incredible journey.

The same applied to me when it came to writing this book. I wrote it while working in a super busy job with heavy responsibilities. So I had to take every little opportunity that came my way to write it. I worked on it while waiting at airports, while riding on trains or while on my phone. I worked on it at 6am and at 1am and at every ungodly hour in between. I just knew I had to use every opportunity I had if I was ever going to get it out. And even though I wrote the first draft in less than four weeks, it took me eleven months to get it print-ready. It doesn't matter how long it's going to take you to reach your goal, you just need to start going and keep going. Eventually you will get there.

Q. But quitting is not that easy. I really get along with my boss and I don't want to disappoint him/her.

It's nothing personal, it's just business. If your employer had to make a business decision that was in the best interest of the organisation but also terminated your position in the company, they wouldn't hesitate. Because it's not personal, it's business. For them it's not about you; it's about the viability of the organisation. And you have got to put yourself first in the same way. They'll survive without you. And you'll survive without them. Remember what the title of this book is? *It's Not You, It's Me!* So make it about you, not the viability of the organisation. Break up with your job if that's what you REALLY want.

Q. But what about the money?

It's perfectly normal to be scared about the financial ramifications of quitting your job. We are all scared of what might happen if our money supply were to dry up. What if we chop off the hand that feeds us? Best to play it safe, right? Well here's the thing. Sometimes the greatest risk is taking no risk at all.

We all have what I like to call a 'money story' and you should figure out what yours is. Mine goes pretty much like this: I had a Christian upbringing and went to a school where money was not seen as a positive thing. I wasn't brought up to respect or love money. I repelled money. In my school it was 'cool' to be poor. And you were treated badly if you were wealthy. So even though my family wasn't *rich*, I always down played my economic background and pretended to be poorer than I was. I worked to earn money but then spent it all so that I didn't have any. But I eventually took that story apart, piece by piece, and realised that this was just a story handed down to me by my peers, my parents and by society. This wasn't my shit. I could write a new story; one where I had a healthy relationship with money. So I did, and it was epic. My new story involved me appreciating the fact that money, like love, is an energy that needs to flow. It involved me realising that I am worthy of being paid for my skills and talents, and that I can earn money doing what I love. And that I can make money while still doing good in the world. And you know what? You can too. You can care and be commercial.

I recommend that you read *Overcoming Underearning: Overcome Your Money Fears and Earn What You Deserve* by Barbara Stanny. It was recommended to me by my delicious friend and colleague Saskia Fraser from Raw Freedom[17]. Barbara's book has plenty of helpful exercises to really help you get a deep understanding of your relationship with money and what you can actually do to improve this relationship.

TRY THIS

Take a piece of paper and write down the absolute minimum amount of money that you need to survive each month. Don't be too drastic, and don't be over-optimistic either. Make sure you cover your expenses and bills. If you want, you can do the strict minimum, or you can do the strict minimum with a bit of extra cash for an occasional shopping trip, a meal out at a restaurant and a visit to the cinema. Don't budget it out so that you can't do anything with your spare time. The idea is to support yourself until you find a life you love, not create a prison for yourself.

Doing this will help you create a clear picture as to how many months you'd be able to survive without a steady source of income. And what's more, it'll also hopefully show you that not having a steady job for a while isn't as bad as you originally thought it would be. For example, if you need £1,500 a month to survive, you'll know that you need to either have £4,500 saved up to survive three income-less months, or that you'll need to find some sort of part-time work that can cover your monthly costs.

When I did this exercise with Elena, one of my clients from my one-to-one coaching programme[18], she realised that all she needed to do was to find five coaching clients per month to cover her costs. That's when she realised she could hand in her resignation notice the very next week!

---

18 For more information on one-to-one support
   visit www.markleruste.com

IF YOU DO WHAT YOU'VE ALWAYS DONE, YOU GET WHAT YOU ALWAYS GOT.

Mark Twain

You have no idea of what might happen on your journey. But if you do nothing about it, you can expect only one thing: the same results you've been having, over and over again.

So if those results haven't been what you've wanted up to now, it's time to change what you're doing. Fast. And as Thomas Jefferson put it, "If you want something you've never had, you must be willing to do something you've never done."

The only real reason you're still sitting in your chair behind your desk bitching about how much you hate your job, or how stuck you currently feel, is because you're scared. Scared that if you do go after what you want, you might not get it. Or worse, scared of doing what you want and realising that you're great at it.

You're scared that you'll struggle financially because you've got too comfortable with your lifestyle and have now become financially dependent on your current source of income. You're scared that you won't be able to provide for your needs or those of your family. You're scared that you'll face rejection again and again. But here's the thing; you've got to keep getting uncomfortable and you have got to put your purpose or mission in front of your comfort.

On the 12th September, 1992, Mae Jemison became the first black woman to travel into space when she went into orbit aboard the space shuttle *Endeavour*. And in her own words, "It's your place in the world; it's your life. Go on and do all you can do with it, and make it the life you want to live."

Dreams don't come true by staying comfortable. They come true by going after what seems impossible, reaching out for what seems to be out of reach, and making things possible.

In her book, *A Return To Love: Reflections on the Principles of a Course in Miracles,* Marianne Williamson talks about our deepest fears in a most compelling way[19]:

> "Our deepest fear is not that we are inadequate. Our deepest fear is that we are powerful beyond measure. It is our light, not our darkness that most frightens us. We ask ourselves, 'Who am I to be

brilliant, gorgeous, talented and fabulous?' Actually, who are you not to be? You are a child of God. Your playing small does not serve the world. There is nothing enlightened about shrinking so that other people won't feel insecure around you. We are all meant to shine, as children do. We were born to make manifest the glory of God that is within us. It's not just in some of us; it's in everyone. And as we let our own light shine, we unconsciously give other people permission to do the same. As we are liberated from our own fear, our presence automatically liberates others."

19 Feel free to replace the word *God* with whatever else it is you
   believe in. This is not meant to be religious propaganda; it is
   meant to share a message that can resonate regardless of whether
   or not you believe in a God.

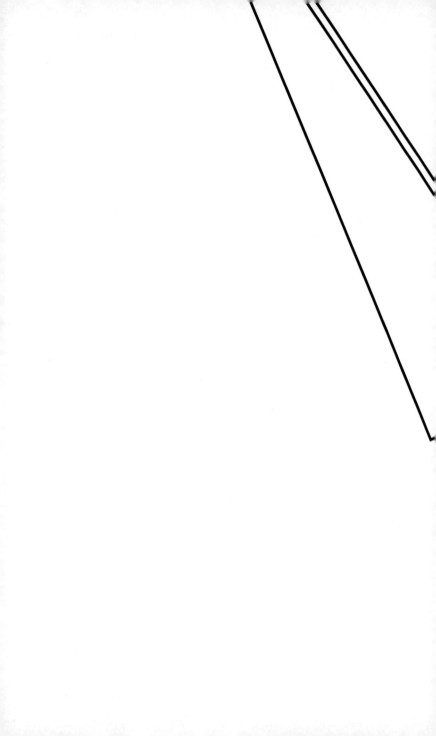

Chapter 8

WHAT TURNS YOU ON?

"The only way to be truly satisfied is to do what you believe is great work. And the only way to do great work is to love what you do. If you haven't found it yet, keep looking and don't settle. As with all matters of the heart, you'll know when you find it."
Steve Jobs

When I discovered Innocent Drinks, a UK-based smoothie company, during my first year at university, I became passionate about what they stood for. I used to preach to everyone I knew about how great they were. I knew, and still know their story inside out. And I could tell it to you like I was part of their team. My final-year marketing teacher at university, Dr Dan Alex Petrovici, told me that I'd be stupid not to apply for a job with them when I graduated. And according to him, Innocent would be stupid to not hire me.

Innocent's founders wrote a book called *A Book About Innocent: Our Story and Some Things We've Learned*, and it is one of my favourite books about starting a conscious business-I strongly recommend you read it. And when you're done with that book, read Michael E Gerber's *The E-Myth Revisited: Why Most Small Businesses Don't Work and What to do About It*. Michael's book will literally be the best business investment you ever make.

Innocent was the organisation I originally really wanted to work for. They were about making life a little bit easier, a little bit better and a little bit healthier. And they did it in a fun and creative kind of way. Richard Reed, one of the founders of Innocent, puts it this way: "Just think of Innocent drinks as your one healthy habit-like going to the gym; but without the communal showers afterwards."

And when you turned one of Innocent's bottles or cartons upside down it read, "Stop looking at my bottom." So in 2011 I applied for one of their positions as a Commercial Executive.

Long story short, I didn't get the job. I lacked the experience in the food and beverage industry. I was so disappointed that I had grown a pair, plucked up the courage to go after my dream job, and been slapped down. Ten months later, when I made my video CV, I re-applied thinking that surely this time they'd see that I was the perfect fit for their team. I was shot down again.

They loved the video CV, but they said I wasn't right for the job I applied for. I was really disappointed and by this point, I was lost and confused. Innocent had been the organisation I really wanted to work for. What was I to do now?

Q. How do I figure out what I actually want to do?
Looking back now, I realise that things really do happen for a reason. Still unclear of what I actually wanted to do, I figured I

might want to work in the advertising industry as it sounded like a viable escape route from my stuck-in-a-rut situation.

A little after the interview with the advertising agency Newhaven in Edinburgh, that I mentioned earlier in Chapter 3, I was standing at a tube station in London. I saw an advertising billboard of a whisky bottle that sported some bullshit slogan, and thought to myself, *there is no way in hell that I would want to push products to consumers that I simply don't believe in.* What I really wanted to do was to make a difference and contribute to the world in a positive way. This had become really clear during my coaching sessions with my coach Roya Ferdows. That's when I dropped the idea of working in advertising and instead started looking at different possibilities that involved social entrepreneurship (something I had learned about while co-ordinating INSEAD's Social Entrepreneurship Programme (ISEP) back in 2011).

Enter Movember, stage left.

Movember[20], the global men's health charity that invites men around the world (with the support of the women in their lives) to grow a moustache for 30 days in November to raise awareness and funds for men's health-particularly prostate cancer, testicular cancer and men's mental health-and the cause I'd spent years campaigning for each Movember as a Mo Bro[21], became the ideal organisation for me to join. It was about having fun, making a difference and doing good.

ENTER

MOVEMBER

Each Movember campaign I went all out and campaigned hard. I'd come up with crazy, creative campaigns. The 2010 Movember campaign posters I made with the help of my friend and photographer Rémi Issaly, from Seven One Three[22], were particularly ballsy.

I released a picture a week during Movember to help me raise as much funding as possible.

20 www.movember.com
21 Mo Bros and Mo Sistas are the men and women around
   the world who take part in Movember each year by signing
   up on Movember.com
22 www.sevenonethree.com

My friend David Arnoux once said, "November is the month I catch colds and block Mark from Facebook." This was due to the amount of traffic, or in David's words, 'spam', I generated during Movember season.

In the middle of my Movember 2011 fundraising campaign I entered a national Bugeï (mixed martial arts) tournament[23] even though I only had two weeks of official training. I thought it would be a great idea to promote the cause and raise funds in a traditionally macho-dominated world of men pounding each other in the face.

Although I was the only (completely) amateur fighter with a moustache, I ended up dislocating my right knee in my second fight. But that's an entirely different story. (For the full story, read my article "Losing My MMA Virginity for Charity"[24] .)

I was later asked by the editor of *Snatch Magazine* to write about the entire experience. I did and it was translated and published in their February 2012 edition; right next to the profile they did on the French former UFC[25] Heavyweight contender, Cheick Kongo.

But I digress. I thought that working for Movember was a silly idea. How the hell would I get in touch with them? And why the hell would they want to hire me anyway? I had no real professional experience working with charities.

But if you don't ask you don't get.

Mark Leruste @MarkLeruste — 16 Jan
@adamgarone Mo Bro to Mo Bro, it's been an honour to champion the November Foubdation. Time to shine! youtu.be/c_PZTAW5pIQ #CVMarkLeruste
▶ View media   ↰ Reply   ↻ Retweet   ★ Favorite   ··· More

adamgarone @adamgarone — 16 Jan
@markleruste - great CV!! Are you based in London?

9:29 PM -19 Jan 12 via TweetDeck Details   ↰ Reply   ↻ Retweet   ★ Favorite   ··· More

And lo and behold, through the power of a simple *tweet* to Adam Garone the CEO and Co-Founder of Movember, I eventually - after weeks of pursuit and gentle harassment - got a face-to-face meeting with JC, one of the other four co-founders of Movember, and was offered the job, on the spot!

"Welcome to the team, mate!" It was the most surreal experience I've ever had. Exhilarating. I had a smile on my face that entire day; all the way from London back to Paris.

I was to join Movember's European team as Country Manager and help launch and develop the foundation across Belgium, France, Spain and Switzerland to help raise funds and awareness for men's health. And the best bit was that although I was to travel across Europe, I would be based in London; something I'd always wanted to be.

Had I not got uncomfortable, I'd still be at my 9-5 job. But landing a position at Movember, just five weeks after my video CV went live, made it all worth it. If I'd never taken action and let the website become just a pipe dream, I would never have started searching for my dream job. I would never have applied to Innocent and Newhaven and I would never have realised that the life of a modern day Don Draper wasn't for me. And I wouldn't have discovered Movember!

Moral of the story? GET UNCOMFORTABLE and TAKE ACTION. If deep down you know that you're in the wrong place and that something doesn't feel quite right, and you know you're not meant to be doing what you're doing; break up with your job, once and for all, and go for what feels right.

---

23 The very same fight tournament that I wrote about in my desperate email to my coach Roya Ferdows in Chapter 2.
24 www.markleruste.com/loosing-my-mma-virginity-for-charity
25 Ultimate Fighting Championship

"There is no passion to be found playing small—in settling for a life that is less than the one you are capable of living."
Nelson Mandela

Q. How will I know what feels right?

You'll know. Trust yourself. Think of it this way: If your heart could talk, what would it tell you? You'll be amazed at how much knowledge you're already sitting on.

LISTEN TO YOUR HEART.

_____

_____

_____

_____

_____

_____

_____

_____

_____

_____

_____

_____

_____

TRY THIS

Close your eyes[26], and take a few deep breaths to help turn down your mind volume for a little while. Next, remember a moment in your life when you felt well and truly happy. It can be something that happened a few days ago, a few months ago, or even a few years ago. Transport yourself to that moment in time. Who is around you? What are you doing? Delve in deep and siphon out every little detail. Are you outside? Are you alone? Get curious and really sink into the experience.

What is it about what you are doing, who you are with, or where you are that makes this moment so special? What is it that makes you feel so alive? Once you've revisited this moment, really soak in the emotion. How are you feeling? And finally, when you feel ready, wiggle your toes and fingers, and slowly bring your attention back to the present moment. Open your eyes.

Take note of the things that had the most impact on you. This is a great way to understand how the moments you feel most alive are usually the moments that your core values in life are being honoured (i.e. what's important to you). Understanding what your core values are is the key to understanding what kind of job you want or what kind of business/lifestyle you want to create.

If you're someone that feels incredibly alive when you're connected to nature, working in an office in an urban city might not be the best scenario for you. Or if you're someone that's at their happiest and most productive when working as a team, working in an environment where you have no social interaction might not be the best choice for you.

When I did this exercise with my client Heather, she discovered that she had a deep connection with the outdoors and helping teams work effectively together. As a result, over the course of our time working together, she went off and developed a retreat in South Africa to help corporate executives and busy city professionals to switch off from their busy lives. They literally have to hand in their smartphones, laptops, etc. upon arrival and re-connect with their true selves. Heather also coupled this retreat with various group activities and philanthropic initiatives and named it the 'Back to Basics Experience'[27].

26 For a guided tutorial on this exercise visit
    www.markleruste.com/book/bonus
27 www.backtobasicsexperience.co.uk

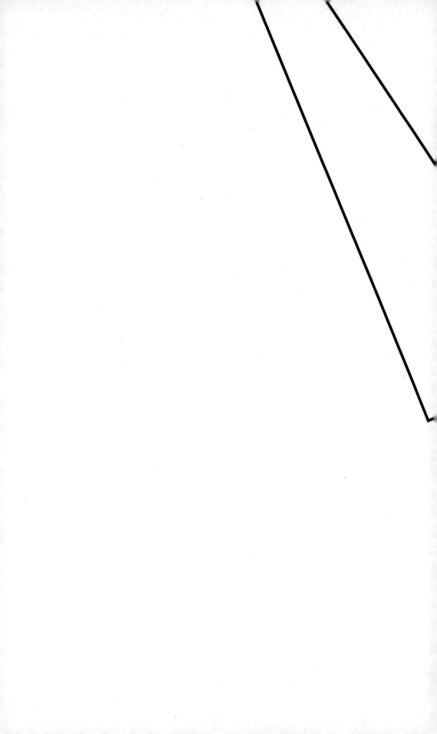

Chapter 9

FILL ME UP!

*"He, who has a strong enough WHY, can bear
almost any HOW."*
Friedrich Nietzsche

We often feel unfulfilled when we start to drift away from what's important to us; our beliefs and our values. If you love spending time with your friends and family and if that human connection holds great meaning to you, and yet you find yourself spending less and less time with them, chances are that you'll start to feel a lot less fulfilled in life. If you love being outdoors and yet you find yourself spending most of your time indoors in front of a computer, chances are that your life will not feel as sweet. In order for us to live our awesome lives we need to know what brings us joy, fulfilment and pleasure and use it as a roadmap-a personal blueprint.

Right now, are you living your life according to somebody else's vision of what your life should be like? Most of the time that so-called 'perfect' picture that you've created; or that you've let other people create for you, the picture that you're probably working yourself miserable to achieve; is probably stopping you from taking the time to smell the roses. It's probably stopping you from telling your boss to stick it so you can work for yourself instead.

Q. How do I become more fulfilled?

Don't get too attached to the negative connotations that come from feeling unfulfilled. Just the simple fact that you're feeling this means that you're alive, which is a pretty good sign. If you stop feeling and start to become numb to the status of your life, you have a much bigger problem on your hands.

Ask yourself what you want your life to look like. In fact, Alex Baisley from the Big Dream Program[28] talks about creating your ideal lifestyle as opposed to searching for your perfect job or business.

Once you have a clear idea of what your ideal lifestyle looks like, you can then focus on building a business (or finding a job) that will support that ideal lifestyle. In fact, most people don't want a dream job; they want a business or a job that will enable them to have an ideal lifestyle.

A lot of the time I speak with clients about what it is they want out of life and the first answer is usually, "I don't know, that's the problem!"

But once you start scratching beneath the surface and delving deep into your core beliefs, the answers will start to appear:

"I want to make a positive impact."
"I want to make a difference."
"I want to be remembered for what I did."

These are great first steps. Now push a little further and start asking yourself what your ideal 'day in the life' would look like.

---

28 www.bigdreamprogram.com

A typical response might be: "I'd wake up and I wouldn't feel the way I feel right now. I'd be full of purpose and full of life, not depressed or lost." But how compelling is this vision? Sure, it feels nice, but does it make you jump out of your seat with excitement to make shit happen? Or is it just a better sounding alternative than what's going on for you right now?

Being pushed away from something will never be as powerful as being drawn towards something. So you've got to create your ideal scenario. It doesn't matter how crazy or how detached it feels from your present situation, you have got to draw, in intricate detail, the perfect day for yourself.

I've noticed that every time I feel down or unfulfilled, it's usually a sign that I am beating myself up about what 'should' be and not what 'is'. Meditation - and yoga - is an amazing practice for this. It hushes that voice inside your head that reminds you that you're feeling like shit and that nothing is going well, and it awakens something much more deeply rooted: inner peace.

"If you are stressed, you are living in the past.
If you are anxious, you are living in the
future. If you are at peace, you are living
in the present."
Lao Tzu

TRY THIS

For the next 10 days, give yourself 10 minutes each day to just sit by yourself and let your thoughts walk freely. Call it meditation, connection, time-out or whatever else that works for you. All that matters is that you do this. Make it a non-negotiable habit like brushing your teeth. In a few days you'll notice how different you feel.

To help you through this challenge, check out a programme called 'Take10'. This is a free, 10-day, 10-minute, guided meditation exercise by Andy Puddicombe, founder of Headspace[29] and dubbed the "Jamie Oliver of meditation" by *The New York Times*. Andy is a former ordained Tibetan monk who's on a mission to demystify mediation and show people the positive effects of taking just a few minutes out of their day to create some head space and be more present.

"Mindfulness is simply being present, in the moment, with an open mind. It's not pretending your worries aren't there-it's learning to be comfortable with them."
Andy Puddicombe

His programme's available to download on iTunes as a free phone app.

29 www.getsomeheadspace.com

While spending time for yourself, reflect on the areas of your life that you can feel good about right now. There's always something, no matter how sublime, going on in everyone's life that they can be grateful for. It could be the love you and your partner share, it could be the sight of your beautiful garden, or it could be your ability to cook a kick-arse raw vegan cheesecake. There is something in your life, right now, that you can be proud of.

Q. Yes, but I still feel like shit. How do I get past that?

I get it. You're lost and it's not easy. I hear you and I feel you. But if you want something to change, you first have to be grateful for what you have.

TRY THIS

Every day, before going to bed, write down five things that you're grateful for. If you're struggling, try harder. It can be anything from, "I'm grateful that it didn't rain today, so I could go outside and have a walk", to "I'm grateful that I have my health and that I am able to move around on my two feet." You can even start a 'gratitude cookie jar'. Write down the good things that happen in your life each day on a piece of paper and add them to the jar. So when you feel down you can pick one out of the jar and remind yourself what you're grateful for. Start flexing your gratitude muscle. Make flexing it every day just as important as breathing. Make it a priority. Or as Marie Forleo calls it, your 'NNT'(Non-Negotiable-Time).

5 things I'm
thankful for:

1.

2.

3.

4.

5.

If you're unhappy at work and you want to change jobs or create a meaningful business of your own, you have got to find something that you love about your current job first. If you feel depressed and down all day, you probably won't have the energy or enthusiasm to keep yourself going after office hours to build your new awesome life. So ask yourself what you love about what you do, and remind yourself of that answer every single day. This will keep you going while you actively seek out new opportunities. People often look over all the amazing experiences they can gain from their current jobs before jumping ship. It's just a question of looking for these valuable experiences in every little thing you do. Then-and this is where the real down and dirty work begins-you have to ask yourself the BIG questions. You have to dig deep.

These will help you to start getting clear about what you really want from life:

What makes you really feel alive?

What makes the time fly by?

Who do you love spending most time with?

What activities do you find yourself drawn to?

What activities make you feel like they stop time itself?

Notice where you come alive:

Is it when you spend time with your friends?

Is it when you're having dinner with peers?

Is it when you're writing an email to your cousins?

Is it when you're going to the cinema?

Is it when you're at an event and listening to an inspiring speaker?

What turns you on?

Make notes. These are all breadcrumbs that leave clues on the path to your purpose; to your *raison d'être*. I use these very questions when I work with teams or individuals, to get clear about what's important to them. This helps them figure out what I've come to call their Value DNA. The things that make them tick and come alive.

TRY THIS

Ask a friend to do the exercise with you. Ask them to take notes on what seems to make you come alive. They can pick up easy signals like your body language-moments when you smile or moments when your posture changes. And if it's over the phone they can notice your tone of voice or level of excitement when you talk about a particular subject. After you've run through the questions ask them to read out what they wrote down and notice what comes up. If you don't have a friend around, you can still do this exercise by recording yourself answering the questions above. You can then listen to your recording and take notes of what *you* notice. Either way, stay curious and keep an open mind. These are the very nuggets that help you figure out what the hell you really love doing.

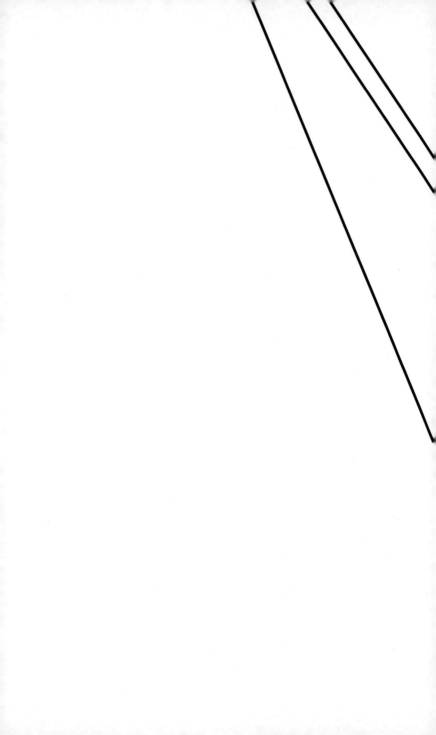

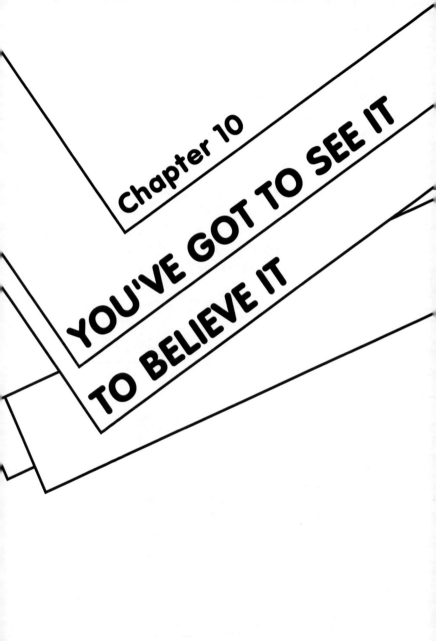

Chapter 10

YOU'VE GOT TO SEE IT

TO BELIEVE IT

"You don't need cheerleaders. You don't need followers. The only person that you need to be successful is yourself."
Eric Thomas

The more I talk with friends, colleagues and clients, the more I realise that almost everyone, at some point, has felt misplaced in their job. It's as if we were all *meant* to do something, before a huge job tsunami came along and swept us all away into jobs that just 'pay the bills'. Who wants to live like that?

I always ask the people I work with, "Why do you get up in the morning?" If your answer to that question is, "I get up in the morning to pay the bills", it's time to take a good look at yourself in the mirror and say out loud what it is you really want to get up in the morning for.

It's okay not to know what it is you want to do. But imagine this: what if you *did* know? Where would you be in five years? Not just in your career, but in life? Would you still be living where you're living? Would you still be earning what you're earning? Would you still be doing what you're doing? If the answers are yes, think again. And go bigger, I dare you.

Take a minute and think about the decisions you would have to have made today to be where you want to be? Now really visualise yourself in the future having achieved all these things that you want. If five years feels too far ahead for you, bring it back to three years. It doesn't even matter if you want to project yourself to just twelve months from now. Whatever the time frame you feel comfortable using, just do it. Now I know what you're thinking: "Cool, I'll do this later when I have a minute." Don't! Remember what I said at the beginning of this book? You have got to take immediate action if you want to see change.

When I first did this exercise, I saw myself having my own TV show and interviewing awesome people who inspire me by making a change in the world. I just knew that I had to do something to promote fellow do-gooders (i.e. Unconventional Hustlers) and give them a voice. I wanted to live in an environment that was

conducive to my creative personality. It became clear in doing this exercise that I had to leave France and move to London, start a blog and launch my coaching business. I did this exercise when I was keen to get in shape. I visualised myself feeling healthy and sexy, and it really helped me through my battle to drop weight and get in shape.

You can read more about my 365 Day Fitness Challenge to inspire busy men to live life in the fit lane at www.mylifeinshape.com as well as read more about my journey to explore the health benefits of switching to a plant-based diet while recovering from a sports injury at www.veganbodychallenge.com.

The important thing is for you to start building yourself a vision to look towards; because when we can see it, we can really start to feel it and truly believe in it. Make this vision as tangible as

2009

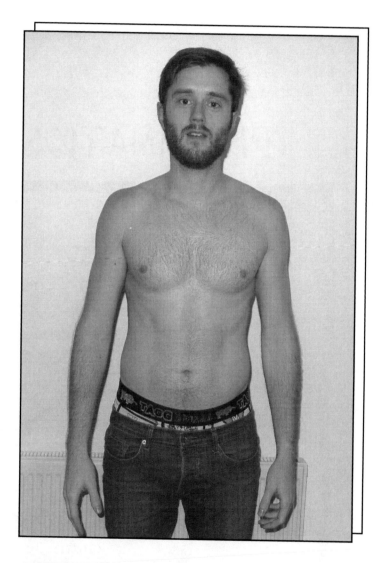

2013

possible. Make it as tasty as possible. It's got to be so juicy that just by closing your eyes and visualising it, you're able to taste how amazing that awesome future tastes. Take the time to do it now.

If you think this is a silly exercise, let me ask you this: What happens to a ship at sea that sets sail without a destination? Sure,

DESTINATION:

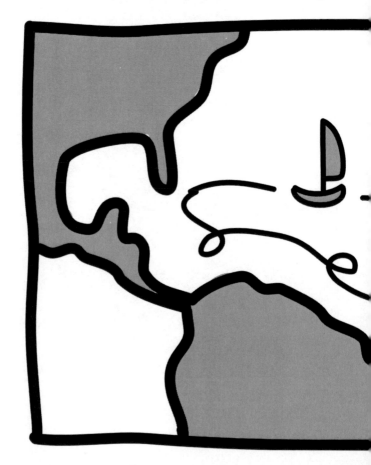

it might feel free for a little while, but eventually it will get lost. It will give up, and most likely, it will disappear or sink. Would you buy a ticket for a cruise not knowing what your destination is, how long it's going to take you to get there, and if you're going to make it there at all?

NOWHERE

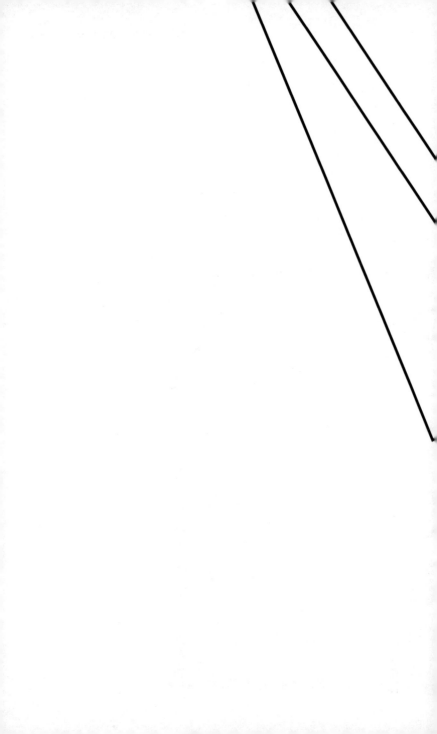

Chapter 11

I DARE YOU

*"Whatever you can do, or dream you can do, begin
it. Boldness has genius, power, and magic in it.
Begin it now."*
W.H. Murray

Your dream job might not even be a 'job'. Your dream job
could very well involve starting your passion-based business.
A business where you get to use your unique skills, talents and
passion to earn a healthy income while making a difference in the
world. This is what becoming an Unconventional Hustler is all
about. And if this resonates with you, I'm 100% in your corner.
Go for it. Take the leap of faith. This is the stuff the very best, big,
hairy, audacious dreams are made of.

In fact, this is what I am most passionate about; helping passionate, creative, buzzing, talented, change-the-world kind of people get out of the starting gates to build their own socially conscious businesses. I help them figure out how they can make a (big) difference, have an impact, get more clients and earn a healthy income while creating the change that they want to see in the world.

In fact, I'm pretty sure that my next book will be just about that. I get so excited working with people who really want to leave a dent in the world and help make it a better place, but just feel stuck in the initial stages. To some of them, marketing, sales and communications can seem like the devil's work—and that's where I come in. I work with these amazing people to show them how to use these tools to amplify their superhero powers and really make a change in the world.

Do you know one of the most common things that I hear from people who have taken the leap of faith into entrepreneurship? They tell me that their only regret is that they didn't take the leap sooner. The only thing holding them back was fear; or should I say, the fear of failure. It's not always easy, but as Chris Guillebeau mentions in his book *The Art of Non-Conformity: Set Your Own Rules, Live the Life You Want and Change the World*, "An entrepreneur is someone who would rather work 24 hours for themselves than work 1 hour for someone else."

And you know what? You might fail, but the sheer act of taking a leap of faith, following your dreams and doing something that really makes a difference will be far more rewarding than anything a safety net could ever provide. It's no secret that when you start chasing your dreams the universe has a way of conspiring to help you along the way; but you have to show up in the first place.

When one of my friends named Rina decided to quit her job at a marketing agency she had no backup plan. All she knew was that what she was doing didn't feel right, and that was enough for her to take action. And guess what? Less than two weeks after leaving her job, without a safety net, she received a phone call from an old colleague of hers asking if she knew anyone available as a freelance social media community manager to help their charity build its online presence. Perfect timing right? Coincidence? Perhaps. But you'd be surprised at the amount of similar stories I hear all the time from people who took the leap of faith and had it pay off. But you have to take action and you have to be wielding a big-arse sword that's ready to slay all your dragons of fear. You in?

"*Twenty years from now you will be more disappointed by the things you didn't do than by the ones you did do. So throw off the bowlines. Sail away from the safe harbor. Catch the trade winds in your sails. Explore. Dream. Discover.*" Mark Twain

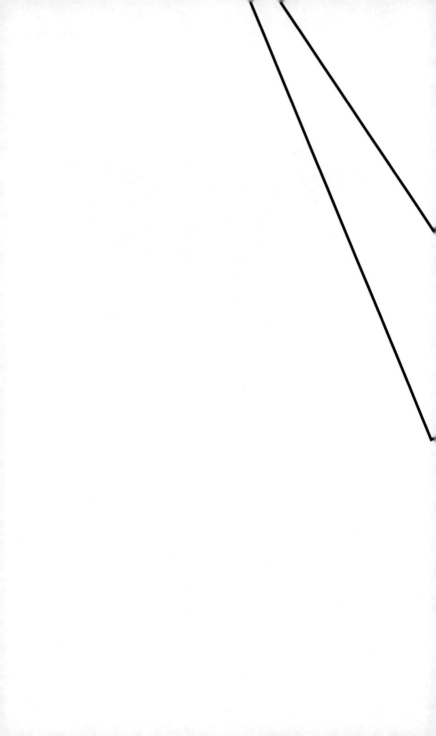

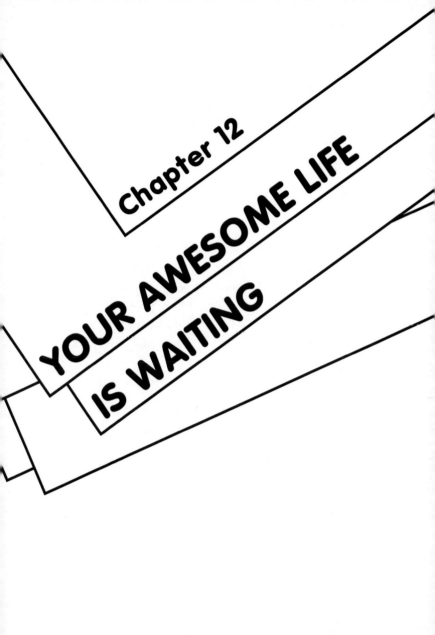

Chapter 12

YOUR AWESOME LIFE
IS WAITING

"Try to help people and make the world a better place. If you strive to do anything remotely interesting, just expect a small percentage of the population to always find a way to take it personally. Fuck 'em. There are no statues erected to critics."
Tim Ferris

Today, my video CV has reached over 40,000 views (and counting) on YouTube and my website www.adreamjobwouldbenice.com has been viewed by thousands of people around the world. I'm still receiving emails and messages from people who have been inspired by it, or want to do something similar to help them land their dream job. And I'm cheering them on 100%.

I've since seen a bunch of video CV businesses pop up online, some of which have contacted me for help and guidance. I've been approached by *AOL Jobs* to be featured in their article on inspiring video resumes and I've been asked to feature in a Finnish job-hunting guide called, "*Työnhakuopas*". I've received awesome testimonials from Amy Gallo of the Harvard Business Review and UFC Hall of Famer and Godfather of Brazilian Jiu-Jitsu, Royce Gracie. I've also been featured on LifeByMe.com[30] along with the likes of Desmond Tutu, Seth Godin and Michael E Gerber, to name just a few and I've recently been asked to become one of the first male contributors for 30ish.me.

If someone tells you that *'it can't be done'* or that *'it's a crazy idea'*, then remember that I heard those very lines while I was creating my video CV.

Don't feel down. Get curious. And although this has been said far too many times in far too many ways, you've got to believe in yourself no matter what. If I had listened to the critics and the negative people around me I never would have gone ahead with my crazy idea to land a dream job with an online campaign and video CV. I never would have joined Movember. I never would have become a certified kick-arse coach. I never would have launched my own business. And I never would have written this book. Once you get over that initial fear bump of, '*But I can't do this!*' you will be amazed at the opportunities that open up for you.

It's time to turn the volume down on that voice inside your head that tells you that you're not good enough, or that you're not able to do it - you know the one I'm talking about - and instead crank the volume up on the even more powerful voice inside your heart; the one that believes in you, no matter what you do.

30 www.lifebyme.com/mark-leruste-courageously

So take these tools and pieces of knowledge that I've given you and plan out your route to your awesome future.

And if while looking at the map you find yourself saying, "Here Be Dragons," don your armour, unsheathe your sword and go face those vile creatures of fear. Get curious. Get adventurous. And then come back and tell me all about your incredible and exciting adventures, yeah?

OH, ONE LAST THING...

*"Make peace with the worst case scenario.
And when you do, then you can fight with a
free heart."*
Gilbert Smith

I want this book to challenge you. I want it to be both a kick in your arse to get up and take action and a hand to hold as you navigate your way through your obstacles and fears. If you're stuck in a job that you hate, or you're feeling unfulfilled and your life pretty much sucks, I hope this is the nudge, cosmic wink or inspiration that you need to break free from your rut, make fear your bitch and live an awesome life.

You have no idea how much awesome shit you're capable of. If someone had told me a year ago that I'd be writing a book about my quest to land my dream job, I'd have laughed in their face. If someone had told me a year ago that I'd be able to quit my job, move abroad, land my dream job at a global men's health charity, have my first feature published in a national magazine, run my first workshop for MBA students, travel to Australia, become a kick-arse and professionally certified coach, launch my own business, get in the best shape of my life, manage three different blogs, have a nurturing long distance relationship, co-lead a retreat in Thailand, give motivational talks, have clients across Europe, Asia, USA and Australia, write and publish a book, get invited by The Skoll Centre for Social Entrepreneurship and Saïd Business School (University of Oxford) to deliver a keynote talk, inspire as many people as possible along the way and win Movember's Global Intrapreneurship Grant award (wow that was a mouthful), I would have told them to check themselves into a mental institution. But what's crazier is that this has all happened.

Playing it safe is not living. It's surviving. So start living.

Ryan Eliason from The Social Entrepreneur Empowerment Series once said that you should "Create your mission and purpose the way you'd like it to be."

So, make it awesome. Make it as awesome as you can possibly imagine, and then go further. Get excited. Get turned on. This is your life we're talking about, what are you waiting for?

I hope this book was helpful and that you were able to take something out of it. Remember, I can't take action for you. Only you can. No one can do push-ups for you. How you do anything is how you do everything.

Start your journey by emailing me (hello@markleruste.com) one action that you're taking right now to create a change in your life. I'm waiting at the other end of your email to give you a high five for getting into gear. Oh yeah!

You can also connect with me on Twitter (@markleruste) using the book's hashtag #ItsNotYouItsMe. And don't forget to drop in with a 'hi' on Facebook (www.facebook.com/markleruste).

"Where the heart is willing, it will find a thousand ways; where it is unwilling, it will find a thousand excuses."
Arien Price

WORK WITH ME

"If you always put limits on everything you do, physical or anything else, it will spread into your work and into your life. There are no limits. There are only plateaus, and you must not stay there, you must go beyond them."
Bruce Lee

Are you still trying to figure out what the fuck you want to do with your life? Or are you still stuck in the initial stages of creating your passion based business that will help you make an impact, earn a healthy income and have fun along the way? Well then, I'm your man.

The best way to work with me is through either signing up for one-to-one support, or joining my group programme (which totally rocks by the way!) or coming along to one of the retreats or workshops that I run. We will work together, and in that time we will make fear your bitch and dance with it. We will embrace failure and together we will create a roadmap heading straight to destination Awesome Life.

If this sounds like you, let's hook up. Let's work together. I want to help you to create your life and work of awesome.

ACKNOWLEDGEMENTS

There are a few people who played a key role in my journey of breaking up with my job and writing this book that I'd like to particularly thank. Here they are in no particular order:

To Denis Duvauchelle; for sticking around through the thick and thin years, and for helping me with all my crazy website ideas. I love you dude. PS Time to put that Red Hot Chilli Peppers concert incident behind us, yeah?

To Mickey Mahut; for giving me the visual voice to express my crazy dream. I'll be forever grateful for the video CV you produced. It never fails to amaze me how talented you are.

To Pamela McNeil; for being the first person to introduce me to coaching and for generously giving me her time to help me reflect on what was important to me, when I needed it most.

To Roya Ferdows; who pushed me to believe in myself, even when I didn't. If it wasn't for Roya I never would have discovered the fascinating world of Co-Active coaching and probably never would have written this book.

To Kiki Deere; for helping me turn some of the dyslexic gibberish on my website www.adreamjobwouldbenice.com into proper English, even though you were busy travel writing in Russia at the time.

To the most awesome, delicious friend, mentor, editor and book coach, Lisa Lister; thank you for being a continuous source of inspiration and for helping me find my voice that had been muted for far too long. You are truly made of magic.

To my amazing friends and colleagues; in particular: Julie Leitz, Angus Fletcher, Naomi Thellier de Poncheville, Kevin Boyd, Saskia Fraser, Heather Orton, Bridget Hunt, Sean Antony, Gus Newsam, Daniel "Pablo" Garay and Leda Sammarco, thank you for taking the time to read the first draft of my book and give me valuable and honest feedback to make this book what it is today.

To the one and only Ben Williamson; for spending St Patrick's day with my final manuscript hunting down typo errors and spelling mistakes. I owe you a LOT of beers.

To Marichiel Boudwin, aka Lilpeanut; who brought this book to life thanks to her amazing talented illustrations. Your creativity, attention to detail and heart-felt customer service is second to none.

To Rina Atienza; for giving me fearless feedback on my book and for taking the time to reshuffle some of the chapters to give it the flow it needed.

To Leonardo Collina; for taking the time to design the book I always wanted and for putting up with my endless changes and edits.

To Lasith Fernando; for handling the final editing and polishing work for this book, despite being incredibly busy taking on the world of heavy metal with his band.

To Alex Denman; for finding the time (and patience) to create an amazing visual identity for Unconventional Hustler. His talent and creative genius blows me away.

To my parents Avril and François; thank you for putting up with my crazy ideas and for loving me regardless of where my feet land. Anything good in me is thanks to you both.

To my brother Johnny Leruste; for helping me keep my feet on the ground by taking the piss out of me once in a while, but always with a smile.

To Carrie Tyler; thank you for your kindness, patience and for editing my CV and cover letter over and over again. Hopefully I'll never need to update my CV ever again.

To Hélène Fyffe; for being so patient with my billion and one projects and most of all, for believing in me no matter what and being my number-one fan.

To my colleagues, teachers, mentors and coaches, past and present; thank you for showing me what's possible and for pushing me beyond reason. Because beyond reason is where the magic takes place.

To my awesome clients; you have inspired me beyond belief and you are the reason that I do the work I do. Keep on dreaming big and no matter what, keep at it and don't give up. The world seriously needs you to live effin' loud.

To everyone else who helped spread my online resume and who shared my video CV; thank you. You truly rock.

To you, the reader, who is about to go out into the world and do the work that matters and the work that's needed; thank you for taking the time to read my book and for taking action despite fear.

ABOUT
THE AUTHOR

Mark Leruste is an award-winning social entrepreneur, men's health activist and author of "*It's Not You, It's Me*" who wholeheartedly believes everyone should pursue their wildest dreams. As a certified coach and self proclaimed Unconventional Hustler, Mark helps unleash frustrated professionals into more fulfilling, entrepreneurial and meaningful careers.

In 2012, his viral video CV, "A Dream Job Would Be Nice" totalled 40,000 views on YouTube and landed him his dream job at Movember, where Mark helped launch and develop the Foundation across four countries.

Over the years, Mark has been featured in *The Wall Street Journal*, *Snatch Magazine*, LifeByMe.com and *The Sunday Telegraph*. He has lived across four continents, generated millions in sales and fundraising, bungee jumped off Victoria Falls, co-founded an online suit-tailoring service for men, competed in a mixed martial arts tournament for charity and became a sponsored vegan athlete overnight.

But Mark's greatest achievement to date might just be that he narrowly escaped a lucrative career in corporate media sales to do the work he's passionate about.

For more information visit www.markleruste.com

Photo Credit: Ollie Grove (www.olliegrove.com)

NOTES

_____

_____

_____

_____

_____

_____

_____

_____

_____

_____

_____

_____

_____

_____

_____

Also by Mark Leruste:

Downloadable e-Books:

Here Be Dragons
Getting Fighting Fit on a Plant-Based Diet

Coming soon in print, for iPad and Kindle:

Message To Movement
The Yo-Yo Journey Of An Entrepreneur